just between us

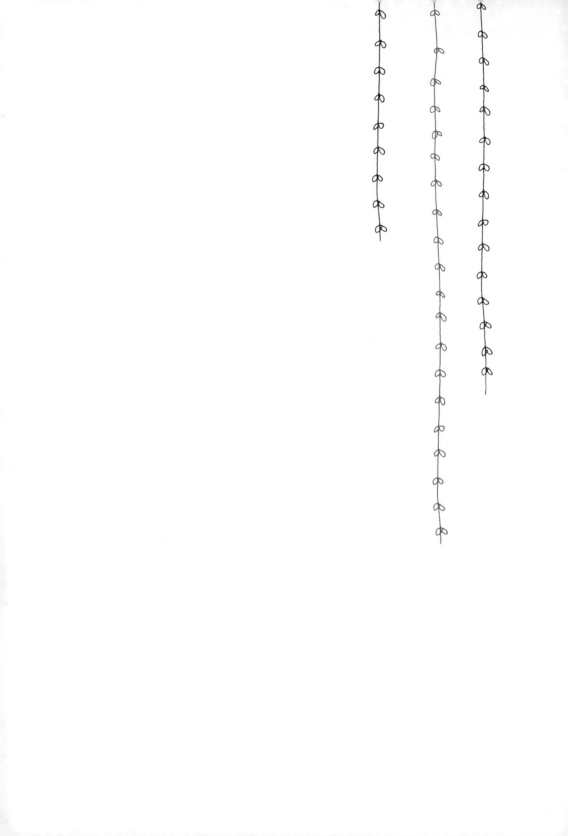

just between us

a no-stress, no-rules journal
for girls and their moms

by Meredith & Sofie Jacobs

chronicle books · san francisco

Design by Molly Baker.
Typeset in Archer.
Illustrations by Molly Baker.
The illustrations in this book were rendered in pen and watercolor.

ISBN 978-0-8118-6895-2

Manufactured by Toppan Excel, Guangzhou City, Guangdong Province,
China, in June 2011

10 9 8 7 6 5

This product conforms to CPSIA 2008.

Chronicle Books LLC
680 Second Street, San Francisco, California 94107

www.chroniclekids.com

this journal belongs to:

Maddie Adams

a daughter's perspective

by Sofie Jacobs

I was in third grade when I developed a crush on the boy who sat across from me in class. He was so cute, so smart, so *perfect*, and best of all there were rumors flying around that *he* had a crush on *me*, too! I did not know what to do. Play hard to get? Follow him around like an abandoned puppy? Ask *him* out? I was beyond confuzzled. So, I asked my friends what to do. They each gave a different reply, and in the end I was way more anxious than before. There was only one solution left.

I had to ask my mom for advice.

No, I couldn't do that! That'd be so embarrassing! I'd never talked to my mom about boys before. What if she yelled at me and said I could never, ever date? What if she gave me the wrong advice? What if she—*gasp*—called *his* mom and together they would laugh about us, saying how cute we were?

No. This could not be an option.

Unfortunately, it had to be.

One day, I finally got up the courage to ask my mom what to do.

"H-h-hi . . . Mom . . ." I stood in the doorway to her office, watching her type animatedly.

"Mmmm . . . ?" she replied, not even looking up from the glowing screen.

"Momthere'sthisguyinmyclassandIreallylikehimandhelikes mebackandIdon'tknowwhattodobecausehe'ssoawesomeandIdon't wanttoscrewthisup," I rushed out in one breath.

For about one whole minute (fifty thousand years to me), she said nothing. I said nothing. Nothing, nothing, nothing. *Twenty-seven seconds. Twenty-eight seconds.*

"Mom?" I asked again.

Forty-five seconds. Forty-six seconds. Forty-seven—

"Mom?"

"Hmm?"

Fifty-five seconds. Fifty-six seconds. Fifty-seven seconds.

"Mom?"

Fifty-nine—

"Huh? Sorry, honey." *Sixty.* "I was preoccupied."

No shoot, Sherlock.

I stood there for a while, my eyes flicking from one side of the room to the other, as if there were a devil and an angel on each side. "Do it!" "No!" "Do it!" "No!"

My mom frowned. "Sweetie . . ." she said, softly. "Sofie, you can tell me. I'll understand, whatever it is."

This is ridiculous, I thought. *My mom and I have a fantabulous relationship. Why can't I just tell her I have a crush on a boy?*

"Sofie . . ."

"It's nothing, Mom." I paused, looking up from my sneakers to see she'd returned to her computer. "Thanks for the help."

"Hmm . . . ?"

I ran to my room and wrote it all in my journal. Sure, it was a little funny, but I was also upset. I'd spent so much time worrying and debating over something that just got a couple of *hmm?*s.

So.

Not.

Worth it.

Anyway, that night I went to cheerleading class. I forget what happened to upset me, I just know that it was something bad. When I got home, I was so upset I couldn't express it in words, so instead I doodled in my journal until I felt calm enough to write. That was when a mental lightbulb went off. Why don't I just write to my mom in a journal? So, I grabbed an empty notebook and two gel pens and told my mom about my idea. I'd write to her in a journal, leave it on her bed, she'd write back . . . TA-DA! Instant mother-daughter communication.

Fast-forward from third grade to now, eighth grade. My mom and I have been journaling for five years now, and have had a blast doing it. Because of the journal I can talk to my mom about all that awful, awkward puberty stuff and not have to face the embarrassment of saying it to her face.

Another thing about the journal is how well we get to know each other through it. Do you know your mom's favorite dinner? How about the name of the first band she saw in concert? Or who she had a crush on in middle school? I don't know about you, but I didn't know that stuff until we started the journal, and it's been a lot of fun being able to get to know my mom better.

But, let's just get something straight: I'm not going to pretend that my mom is supermom and I'm superdaughter. Because we're *not*. We do fight sometimes! Which is another bonus about the journal—I can talk to my mom about stuff when I'm annoyed or mad at her, and we can work it out without getting upset all over again.

One time we got into a fight about my little brother. I love my brother and all, but sometimes I feel like he has it easier than I do. Like, when he gets a B on a math test, it's "good job!" but when I do, it's "why didn't you study harder?" And it seems like I'm always the one letting the dog out and clearing the table after dinner while he gets to go play Guitar Hero or something. So, I told my mom how I felt and she got mad. "Your brother does not get more attention than you, and does not have fewer chores than you, and does not get less of a hard time when he doesn't do well in school. . . ." Blah, blah, blah. I felt like since my mom got mad, I couldn't talk to her about it again. So I wrote to her in the journal. And it really helped! My mom and I were able to talk it out without blowing up and getting in a big argument. Now my mom and I don't even need to use the journal to talk things out when we get into fights. The journal has helped us listen better and understand each other's perspective. I think we've become closer because of it. And it's been tons of fun along the way.

I'm really thankful for the journal, because now I know that my mom will always hear me out, and that even if she can't write back right away, I can always say what I need to say. With the journal, if I suddenly get an upsetting text or IM from a friend, I can tell my mom what happened and how I feel right away, instead of having to wait to tell her when she gets home. Even when she's busy or at a meeting or something, I know that I can always say what I need to say in the journal, and she will always get back to me. I think if we didn't have our journal, my life and my relationship with my mom would be a lot different. I'm really happy it's not.

a mother's perspective

by Meredith Jacobs

"Why don't you just talk?" my neighbor asked when I told her about keeping a journal with my daughter Sofie.

That made me think. Was she right? Should we "just talk"? Is talking better? Is journaling . . . avoiding?

And then I realized that Sofie and I do talk. Talking and journaling are not mutually exclusive—they are mutually beneficial. Journaling with my daughter serves to further strengthen and deepen and widen our relationship—it's one more tool in our toolbox. And besides . . . it was Sofie's idea.

I'd love to take credit. One would guess that, I, "Supermom," who was always the one to ask the deliverymen to leave the box the refrigerator came in so we could turn it into a puppet theater, would have been the one to think of keeping a journal with my daughter, but no, it was her idea.

I remember the moment. She was nine. One night she came home from cheerleading class and went right to her room. She was quiet at dinner. I kept asking, "What's wrong?" and she would answer, "Nothing." (Yeah, right, "nothing.")

Finally, she asked me to come in her room. I can still see her standing there, me in the doorway, her telling me that there were times she wanted to talk to me, but felt too embarrassed or silly to say whatever it was out loud. She asked if we could keep a journal together so that she could write to me and then I could write her back.

I jumped at the idea—who wouldn't? We found a spiral notebook and declared it our journal that no one else could see (including her dad—she made me promise, promise, promise not to show even him). And thus began our written relationship. Funny how I remember what she wrote, but not exactly how I responded. In a way, it almost didn't matter what exactly we wrote about. What really made me happy was that this journal allowed us to talk, even when she didn't feel like talking.

We've been journaling ever since. Our entries are not always serious—not always about "teen angst." She recently wrote that she loves how the house smells when her father and I are dressed up to go out. I smiled and I shared memories of watching my mother putting on makeup before a party and smelling the perfume she saved for special occasions. I love those entries when we're just sharing stories, dreams, ideas.

I love that we communicate a little differently when we write because we have time to think. My mind often wanders when I write, so I think I share even more than I do when we talk. It's quite possible that she "hears" me better when I write. And, she's braver when she writes. Honestly, there are times Sofie writes that she's kind of mad at me. I don't think she would have the nerve to say these words to me out loud. And I don't know how open I would be to hearing them. Sometimes writing and reading gives us just enough distance to be honest.

I'll never forget the time she told me she was angry with me because she thought I was easier on her brother than I was on her. I was happy that she told me, that she didn't let the resentment fester. I was also annoyed. Seriously, I'm an *awesome* mom. How in the world could she find fault with me?! But because I was reading it, I was able to step back and consider if there was truth to what she wrote. More important than whether it was true, her feelings were honest. I needed to address how she felt without being defensive.

I actually didn't know until I read a draft of her introduction for this book that one of the reasons she wanted to journal was because sometimes I was too busy on my computer or on the phone and wasn't available when she wanted to talk to me. It's true. Parents aren't always available when our children want to talk. We *can't* always be. But because of the journal, conversations won't be lost while she waits.

I think this is especially important as we both become busier. Already I'm seeing a difference in her schedule since we started our journal. The time we have to just sit and talk becomes less and less every year. And yet, as she moves further into her teenage years, I need her to know that she will always have a way of communicating with me. A vehicle to express her feelings and thoughts, her worries and frustrations. And a way of sharing them with me.

Writing in our journal has also made it easier and more natural to e-mail, text, and IM with each other. Now that Sofie is a full-fledged middle schooler, I see how much kids today communicate through writing. They don't call each other, they text. It's exciting to see how our journal paved the way for her to "talk" to me as she does to her friends and, while I know it's still several years away, I can already imagine continuing our journal in electronic form when she's in college.

So much is happening to girls at this age. And, unfortunately, it's happening so much faster than it used to. In the few years Sofie and I have journaled, our entries have gone from brothers to boys, playdates to puberty. It's all happening now. Sometimes Sofie seems so mature and confident

I forget everything she's navigating. I'm reminded that she's still a young girl trying to understand her physical and emotional changes when I read an entry in which she asks about something I know she'd be too embarrassed to say—and absolutely mortified to have to listen to my answer. I know I didn't have the nerve to talk to my mom about this stuff. Writing makes it easier to broach some topics—but I have found that once we've "talked" on paper, continuing the conversation in person is comfortable.

Sofie and I are wonderfully close. Would we have been even without the journal? Perhaps. But I know we've shared more than we would have without our written conversations. Even when her entries are quizzes—when she asks me everything from my favorite song to the latest I've slept in and why—she's learning about me as a person (not just her mom). I think this allows her to relate to me differently. And I'm then given the opportunity to ask her questions. I learn everything from her favorite color to what she's looking for in a boy.

Whenever I speak to groups of moms, the story of our journal comes up and I see women jotting down notes to "buy a journal." I think it's an idea that just makes sense. I've even heard from moms of older teens who journaled with their kids. One mom whose son was going through a difficult time gave him a journal and started a separate one for herself. Every so often they would sit on the floor, back-to-back, and read out loud to each other from their individual journals. This was their way of sharing what they were each going through, and as a result, they were able to connect more intimately.

I hope you find as much meaning in the journal you are starting as Sofie and I have found in ours. I am so grateful—grateful not only for what we are sharing now, but for the time capsule we are constructing. I think about Sofie as a little girl—it wasn't all that long ago, but already I've forgotten so much. What she sounded like and what we talked about . . . what made her laugh and what made her cry: the details dance around the edges of my memory. I want to pull them closer. In the blink of an eye, she'll be grown. But I know we have our journal. And I can imagine one day, years from now, finding it and reading it and instantly being transported back. Everything, from what we're writing about to her handwriting and the expressions she uses, captures her in this moment.

More powerful than a photograph is the life I'm writing with my daughter.

Ideas for Getting Started

This journal includes writing prompts to help get the conversation going, plus fun ideas for making lists and drawing pictures. There's also plenty of free space for writing about day-to-day experiences and whatever's on your minds—and two ribbons for marking your places. Before getting started, you might want to sit down to talk about how the process will work for you. We developed our idea at a bookstore that happens to serve amazing chocolate cake. We sat down with two forks and a huge piece of cake, and fleshed out our plan for the journal. It might seem unnecessary to have this talk, since the process should be intuitive, but it's a good idea to make sure you're on the same page. The following section suggests a few ideas to help you along the way.

You Need to Decide a Couple of Key Things

1. **Who is allowed to see the book?** You have to honor this—trust is a key component to the success of this journal.

2. **How will you pass the journal back and forth?** We use our night tables, but we always let each other know when we've left it, as in "I wrote something new in the journal and left it on your night table." We learned this the hard way after the journal sat, unread, buried under a mountain of other books and magazines!

3. **When can you expect a response?** Sometimes it's hard to find time to write back (moms get tired, daughters get homework). Think of a way to let each other know how important a response is. Sometimes, in the middle of a particularly long entry, Sofie will write "This question is actually kinda serious, please respond." Maybe put a sticky flag on the page to highlight "response needed ASAP," like you would flag an e-mail, or if it's not urgent you can simply say, "I wrote something, but get back to me whenever." (Moms—try not to wait too long—she is trying to communicate!)

4. **How are you going to address each other?** Dear You . . . Love, Me? Dear Mommy? Dear Daughter? Dear [Insert Name Here]? This may seem like an unnecessary step but it does help set the tone.

5. **What are you going to write with?** Seriously. You may want to pick out a special pen you can keep clipped to the binding of the book. Keeping a pen attached also makes it easier to respond and saves time on rummaging through various drawers to find

one! Buy a box of colored pencils or crayons for illustrating your entries. You also might want to discuss handwriting. Although you don't want to worry about penmanship or have this seem like a school writing assignment where "neatness counts," you have to remember that someone else will be reading what you've written—so make it legible.

Guidelines

1. **What's written in the journal, stays in the journal.** If either of you writes that she does not want to discuss an entry outside of the journal, you have to abide by that and respect the fact that it is a journal-only topic for whatever reason.

2. **The journal is your space to say anything.** Don't get mad. Moms, your daughter has to feel like she can tell you anything. If she thinks you'll get mad or punish or lecture her for something, she won't write. Same goes for daughters. Moms have to know they can be honest and you won't pout or stomp around the house if you don't like what you read. This is about open and honest communication. It won't work if you are worried about editing yourself.

3. **Be honest.** Did we already say that? Well, it's important, so we'll say it again . . . be honest.

4. **Remember to have fun.** The journal is not just about discussing sensitive issues; it's about adding another layer to your relationship. Every once in a while, write about something silly. Tell a story, draw

a picture, or list the movie stars or musicians you have (or had) crushes on.

5. **Most important: Never forget how much you love each other.** Treasure this book and the opportunity it gives you. Think how much closer you will become and how in many, many, many years, you will both have it as a very special snapshot of what life was like between you right now.

Twenty things about me

1. Last thing I ate ....
2. Last person I talked to ....
3. If every food were healthy, I'd eat ....
4. Favorite veggie ....
5. Favorite TV show ....
6. Favorite movie ....
7. Favorite song ....
8. Favorite book ....
9. Favorite year in school ....
10. Favorite word ....
11. Favorite holiday ....
12. Something I'd do if I knew I'd never fail ....
13. Guilty pleasure ....
14. I want to go to ....
15. I hate ....
16. I love ....
17. I believe in ....
18. A trend I love to hate ....
19. Favorite thing about my daughter ....
20. Favorite thing to do with my daughter ....

mother

July 31 2013

Twenty things about me

1. Last thing I ate... *Pancakes* ....

2. Last person I talked to ....

3. If every food were healthy, I'd eat *candy* ....

4. Favorite veggie ....

5. Favorite TV show ....

6. Favorite movie ....

7. Favorite song ....

8. Favorite book ....

9. Favorite year in school ....

10. Favorite word ....

11. Favorite holiday ....

12. Something I'd do if I knew I'd never fail ....

13. Guilty pleasure ....

14. I want to go to ....

15. I hate ....

16. I love ....

17. I believe in ....

18. A trend I love to hate ....

19. Favorite thing about my mom ....

20. Favorite thing to do with my mom ....

daughter

The first day I was home alone with you after you were born, I remember feeling ....

....

....

....

....

When you lost your first tooth, I remember thinking ....

....

....

....

....

On your first day of school, I remember ....

....

....

....

....

And other firsts ....

....

....

....

....

....

....

mother

My earliest memory is ....

....

....

....

....

....

....

....

When I was little I thought that ....

....

....

....

....

....

....

....

My favorite memory of you and me is ....

....

....

....

....

....

....

....

....

....

daughter

Things I talked to my mom about when I was your age ....

....

....

....

....

....

....

....

....

....

....

....

mother

Things I wish I'd been able to talk to her about ....

....

....

....

....

....

....

....

....

....

....

....

....

Things I like talking to you about ....

....

....

....

....

....

....

....

....

....

....

....

....

Things I find it hard to talk to you about ....

....

....

....

....

....

....

....

....

....

....

....

....

daughter

free spaces

free space

free space

free space

What I wanted to be when I grew up ....

....

....

....

....

....

....

....

....

....

mother

What really happened when I grew up and why ....

....

....

....

....

....

....

....

....

....

....

....

Three things I might want to be when I grow up and why

1. ....
....
....
....
....
....
....
....

2. ....
....
....
....
....
....
....
....

3. ....
....
....
....
....
....
....
....

daughter

What I was like when I was a daughter your age ....
....
....
....
....
....
....
....
....
....
....
....
....
....
....
....
....
....
....
....
....
....
....
....
....

mother

What I'd be like if I were a mom ....

....

....

....

....

....

....

....

....

....

....

....

....

....

....

....

....

....

....

....

....

....

....

....

                              ....

                              ....

daughter

A drawing of my dream outfit

(And where I'd wear it and what I'd do in it)

mother

A drawing of my dream outfit

(And where I'd wear it and what I'd do in it)

daughter

free space

free space

Who my friends were when I was growing up ....

....

....

....

....

....

....

....

How my friendships have changed ....

....

....

....

....

....

....

....

What I've learned about friendship ....

....

....

....

....

....

....

....

mother

My best friends are ....

....

....

....

....

....

....

....

What I look for in a friend ....

....

....

....

....

....

....

....

The challenges I face in my friendships ....

....

....

....

....

....

....

....

daughter

Here's the story of the most embarrassing thing that happened to me at school (and how I got through it) ....

....

....

....

....

....

....

....

....

....

mother

....

....

....

....

....

....

....

....

....

....

....

....

....

Here's the story of the most embarrassing thing that happened to me at school (and how I got through it) ....

....

....

....

....

....

....

....

....

....

....

....

....

....

....

....

....

....

....

....

....

....

....

....

....

daughter

my top 10 favorite songs

1. ....

2. ....

3. ....

4. ....

5. ....

6. ....

7. ....

8. ....

9. ....

10. ....

mother

my top 10 favorite songs

1. ....

2. ....

3. ....

4. ....

5. ....

6. ....

7. ....

8. ....

9. ....

10. ....

daughter

free space

free space

free space

My novel sold for $50K!

What is it about?

mother

They're filming the story of my life!

Who are the stars and what's it about?

....
....
....
....
....
....
....
....
....
....
....
....
....
....
....
....
....
....
....
....
....
....
....
....
....
....
....

daughter

A funny story about me when I was your age ....

....
....
....
....
....
....
....
....
....
....
....
....
....
....
....
....
....
....
....
....
....
....
....

mother

The funniest thing that has happened to me is ....

....

....

....

....

....

....

....

....

....

....

....

....

....

....

....

....

....

....

....

....

....

....

....

....

daughter

Before I fall asleep, I think about

I often dream about

The first thing I think of when I wake up is

mother

Before I fall asleep, I think about ....

....

....

....

....

....

....

....

I often dream about ....

....

....

....

....

....

....

....

The first thing I think of when I wake up is ....

....

....

....

....

....

....

....

....

daughter

free space

free space

free space

free space

Have you ever let fear stop you from doing something you wanted to do? Tell me about it.

mother

Have you ever let fear stop you from doing something you wanted to
do? Tell me about it. ....

....

....

....

....

....

....

....

....

....

....

....

....

....

....

....

....

....

....

....

....

....

daughter

My greatest achievement ....

....

....

....

....

....

....

....

My biggest regret ....

....

....

....

....

....

....

....

A decision I made that changed everything ....

....

....

....

....

....

....

....

....

My greatest achievement ....

....

....

....

....

....

....

....

My biggest regret ....

....

....

....

....

....

....

A decision I made that changed everything ....

....

....

....

....

....

....

....

daughter

Love it! or Ew! No!

Love it!   Ew! No!

mother

Reality television ....

Flare jeans ....

Sushi ....

Poetry ....

Rock music ....

Texting ....

Dancing ....

Singing ....

Acting ....

Sitcoms ....

Vampires ....

Rainy days ....

Gummy worms ....

Techno music ....

Thunderstorms ....

Puppet shows ....

Ghost stories ....

Water parks ....

Computer games ....

Exercise ....

Mayonnaise ....

Dangly earrings ....

Road trips ....

Puppies ....

80s movies ....

Love it!   Ew! No!

....
....
....
....
....
....
....
....
....
....
....
....
....
....
....
....
....
....
....
....
....
....
....
....

daughter

free space

free space

free space

free space

A note to my past self

mother

daughter

A song about my daughter

(set to a popular song tune)

A song about my mom

(set to a popular song tune)

daughter

How you and I are the same ....

....

....

....

....

....

....

....

How we are different ....

....

....

....

....

....

....

....

Things I admire about you ....

....

....

....

....

....

....

....

mother

How you and I are the same ....

....

....

....

....

....

....

....

How we are different ....

....

....

....

....

....

....

....

Things I admire about you ....

....

....

....

....

....

....

....

daughter

free space

free space

mother

Growing up, I looked like ....
....
....
....
....

I dressed like ....
....
....
....
....

I felt like ....
....
....
....
....

Do I think we would have been friends? ....
....
....
....
....
....

How I would describe my appearance ....

....

....

....

....

....

....

....

....

My favorite feature ....

....

....

....

....

....

....

What I wish I could change about myself ....

....

....

....

....

....

....

....

....

daughter

My first crush (and what I've learned since!) ....

....

....

....

....

....

....

....

....

....

....

....

....

....

....

....

....

....

....

....

....

....

....

....

....

mother

What I need to know about crushes and dating ....

....

....

....

....

....

....

....

....

....

....

....

....

....

....

....

....

....

....

....

....

....

....

....

daughter

Questions I have for you

1. ....

2. ....

3. ....

4. ....

5. ....

6. ....

7. ....

8. ....

9. ....

10. ....

mother

Questions I have for you

1. ....

2. ....

3. ....

4. ....

5. ....

6. ....

7. ....

8. ....

9. ....

10. ....

daughter

free space

My craziest dream

....
....
....
....
....
....
....
....
....
....

mother

Daughter's analysis

....
....
....
....
....
....
....
....
....
....
....
....

My craziest dream ....

....

....

....

....

....

....

....

....

....

....

....

Mom's analysis ....

....

....

....

....

....

....

....

....

....

....

....

daughter

Shh! Something even my best friend doesn't know ....

mother

Shh! Something even my best friend doesn't know ....

....

....

....

....

....

....

....

....

....

....

....

....

....

....

....

....

....

....

....

....

....

....

....

....

daughter

A drawing of my dream room

(doesn't have to be a bedroom—
could be a kitchen, library, sunroom, fab closet)

mother

A drawing of my dream room

(doesn't have to be a bedroom—
could be a kitchen, library, sunroom, fab closet)

daughter

free space

free space

free space

Things I would love for us to do together

1. ....

2. ....

3. ....

4. ....

5. ....

6. ....

7. ....

8. ....

9. ....

10. ....

mother

Things I would love for us to do together

1. ....

2. ....

3. ....

4. ....

5. ....

6. ....

7. ....

8. ....

9. ....

10. ....

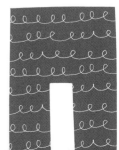

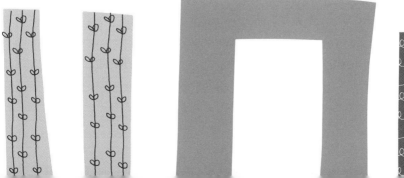

What I imagined it would be like having a daughter ....

....

....

....

....

....

What I couldn't imagine ....

....

....

....

....

....

What I especially love about us ....

....

....

....

....

....

What I hope we can do better ....

....

....

....

....

....

What I love about having you as my mom ....

....

....

....

....

....

....

....

What I don't love as much ....

....

....

....

....

....

....

....

What I hope we can do better ....

....

....

....

....

....

....

....

daughter

If I could do one crazy thing without consequences, it would be ....

....

....

....

....

....

If I could have any superpower, it would be ....

....

....

....

....

....

If I could travel anywhere in the universe, it would be to ....

....

....

....

....

....

If I could live during any time and be anything I wanted, it would be

....

....

....

....

....

If I could do one crazy thing without consequences, it would be ....

....

....

....

....

....

If I could have any superpower, it would be ....

....

....

....

....

....

....

If I could travel anywhere in the universe, it would be to ....

....

....

....

....

....

If I could live during any time and be anything I wanted, it would be

....

....

....

....

....

daughter

free space

In five years, I want to be ....
....
....
....
....
....
....
....
....
....
....
....
....
....
....
....
....
....
....
....
....
....
....
....
....
....
....

mother

In five years, I want to be ....

....

....

....

....

....

....

....

....

....

....

....

....

....

....

....

....

....

....

....

....

....

....

....

....

daughter

A drawing of what's in my purse

mother

A drawing of what I think is in your backpack

A drawing of what's in my backpack

A drawing of what I think is in your purse

daughter

My favorite sport to play (or why I don't like sports) ....

....

....

....

....

....

....

The sport I wish I could play, but can't ....

....

....

....

....

....

....

....

How sports and exercise make me feel about myself and my body

....

....

....

....

....

....

....

....

mother

My favorite sport to play (or why I don't like sports) ....

....

....

....

....

....

....

....

The sport I wish I could play, but can't ....

....

....

....

....

....

....

....

How sports and exercise make me feel about myself and my body

....

....

....

....

....

....

....

....

daughter

free space

free space

free space

How I felt about school when I was your age ....

....

....

....

....

....

How my parents handled my schooling ....

....

....

....

....

....

What I want you to know about school and getting into college

....

....

....

....

....

My greatest learning experience (in school or out) ....

....

....

....

....

....

mother

What I love about school ....

....

....

....

....

....

What I don't love about school ....

....

....

....

....

....

How I feel about my grades ....

....

....

....

....

....

My greatest learning experience (in school or out) ....

....

....

....

....

....

daughter

How I handle feeling overwhelmed ....

....

....

....

....

....

What I wish I could spend more time doing ....

....

....

....

....

....

What I wish you could spend more time doing ....

....

....

....

....

....

What I'd do if I could do anything in the world ....

....

....

....

....

....

mother

How I feel about the number of activities I'm involved in ....

....

....

....

....

....

What takes up too much of my time ....

....

....

....

....

....

What I wish I could spend more time doing ....

....

....

....

....

....

What I'd do if I could do anything in the world ....

....

....

....

....

....

daughter

Books I loved that I hope you'll read

1. ....

2. ....

3. ....

4. ....

5. ....

6. ....

7. ....

8. ....

9. ....

10. ....

Books that I hated to see end

1. ....

2. ....

3. ....

4. ....

5. ....

6. ....

7. ....

8. ....

9. ....

10. ....

daughter

free space

What I loved to draw when I was your age

mother

What I love to draw

daughter

mother

I love ....
....
....
....
....
....
....
....

I wish ....
....
....
....
....
....
....
....

I hope ....
....
....
....
....
....
....
....

I love ....
....
....
....
....
....
....
....

I wish ....
....
....
....
....
....
....
....

I hope ....
....
....
....
....
....
....
....
....

daughter

make your
own list

mother

1. ....

2. ....

3. ....

4. ....

5. ....

6. ....

7. ....

8. ....

9. ....

10. ....

make your own list

1. ....

2. ....

3. ....

4. ....

5. ....

6. ....

7. ....

8. ....

9. ....

10. ....

daughter

What I've learned from our journal

mother

What I've learned from our journal ....
....
....
....
....
....
....
....
....
....
....
....
....
....
....
....
....
....
....
....
....
....
....
....
....
....
....
....
....

daughter

free space

free space

free space

free space

free space